The Blood in Our Veins, The Roots to Our Trees

A Southeast Asian Anthology

The Blood in Our Veins, The Roots to Our Trees: A Southeast Asian Anthology

Editor:

Anh-Vy Phan

Alyssa Ranola

Copyright © 2021 by Southeast Asian Student Coalition

Website:

https://www.ocf.berkeley.edu/~sasc/

Published by:

EASTWIND BOOKS OF BERKELEY

2066 University Avenue

Berkeley, CA 94704

www.AsiaBookCenter.com

email: eastwindbooks@gmail.com

Cover design by Gabby Nguyen.

Eastwind Books of Berkeley is a registered trademark of Eastwind Books of Berkeley

ISBN: 9781734744026 (Paperback)

ISBN: 9781734744057 (Ebook)

Table of Contents

Dedications

"To QTViet Cafe Collective, my paternal grandfather, my past self and future self, and all my friends who have helped me when I could not continue to move forward." — Phibi Tran

"I would like to dedicate my art piece to my friends from SAFE (Southeast Asians Furthering in Education) community at UC Davis, California, as well as friends I made through SASC SI 2019, and most importantly, I also want to dedicate this piece to Tatum Phan. Because of her, I was able to find a loving community." — Jennifer Hua

"This is for my younger sister, who continuously shows and teaches me compassion. This is for my mom, who loves me unconditionally. This is for my friends who have challenges and conversed with me to grow. This is for my best friends who have dared to dream with me. This is for my mentors who are bringing me to the threshold of my mind." — Riss Myung

"I want to dedicate my work to my parents, uncle, and cousin for their hard work, and for their patience, openness towards me as a Filipino American finding her way. I also appreciate my brother, who is doing the same." — Alyssa Ranola

"For Anne Parris." — Anastasia Doanh Trinh Le

"I dedicate my pieces to my mother, who took on the role of being two parents in one at a young age, to my maternal grandmother, who shows me that love has no boundaries, to my uncle, who gave me ice-cream when I was down, to my brother, who I still struggle to hold a conversation with but love unconditionally, and to my friends and community both back home in Santa Ana and at UC Berkeley who constantly help me redefine love, happiness, and home." — Anh-Vy Phan

"Shoutout to my housemate Austin!" -Gabby Nguyen

"For my grandfather." -Prinston Pan

Preface

Anh-Vy Phan

Thank you to everyone at Southeast Asian Student Coalition, Asian Pacific American Student Development, Eastwind Books of Berkeley, and the broader Southeast Asian and Asian American and Pacific Islander community for supporting this project. This is the first anthology that SASC has produced in five years, and it has been incredibly difficult, but nevertheless fruitful, and would not have been made possible without you all.

The SASC Anthology was born out of frustration, pain, and the need for representation in academia. In 2007, Dr. Khatharya Um, Associate Professor of Asian American Studies at the University of California, Berkeley, brought forth a project for the Southeast Asian Student Coalition that focused on documenting the stories and memories of first-generation Southeast Asian refugees through creative writing. At the time, Southeast Asian narratives were highly underrepresented. Professor Um and the SASC Community wanted to create something that would stand against time; something that would keep our and our ancestors' stories alive, both in and outside of the classroom.

What started out as a documentation of first-generation Southeast Asians became that of the 1st, 2nd, 3rd, and even 4th generation Southeast Asian Americans. Spearheaded by Maurice Seaty and Tracy Nguyen in the early beginnings and later picked up by Binly Phounsiri and Brian Pham, SASC Anthology has been able to publish its first chapbook in 2009-2010 with a committee led by co-chairs Son Chau and Dat Phan.

This year marks the 46th year of the Southeast Asian Diaspora's Anniversary. It's been 46 years since our people's mass exodus from Southeast Asia, but for some, the war never left. There are those who still struggle with a plethora of mental health struggles, intergenerational trauma, deportation, environmental racism, and so many other issues that are not publicized in the media. Our struggles and our people are continued to be made invisible and erased from American history and media, but not anymore.

The second, third, fourth and counting generation of Southeast Asians in America will continue to rise, to advocate for our communities, and fight to be seen, heard, and understood. This anthology is an effort of that.

This anthology is a collection of second generation Southeast Asian-Americans' sorrows, struggles, and heart. We offer these pieces of ourselves to our community in hopes of promoting healing, growth, and prosperity.

Word Bender

Riss Myung

Grew up wanting to be a New York Times Best Selling author

but I catch myself more times often than not as a mentor

with rhymes littered on the floor / never picked up past the door

Used to want to be an advocate wishing I was Hecate

spinning spells up wishing wells

wishing I could articulate what I wanna mitigate

Now I just say fuck these reactionary arguments

that perpetuate the same old forms of oppression

slapped on social justice terms

Used to think half this half that part this part that

Used to say I'm a half East Asian and a half Southeast Asian woman

Thinking that I'm mixed / not mixed enough a cultural charlatan

Why am I fragmented / focusing on pieces to be distributed / feeling so restricted

Moving so disjointed / all this thinking shouldn't be so complicated / it just means the diaspora's expanded

Still seeing parts of my identity folded up like origami

Made every crease run like a beast / out for my blood

Don't they know I grow in the mud?

Grew up thinking I was gonna be a physician

But baby lemme tell ya with words I'm a magician

With this outside education / my spirit has now awaken / it feels so utterly refreshing

All I had to do was ask who really who benefits from identity politics and from participating in the games of oppression olympics

Who is to deem what pieces of me are not acceptable

Pieces that are outside of my control / unlike these syllables

So know I'm just whole, I'm raising, I'm both East and Southeast Asian

I'm my own prodigy

Hit ya with words you didn't think was in the dictionary

In my Zodiac got fangs and stingers

It's an indicator that I'm leading no longer loading

Visioning something radical beyond the gradient

I dare to day-dream in this ordinary

Inspired by what I'm reading and seeing

That no one is one's jurisdiction

Made friends with the librarian / but wasn't a valedictorian

Grew up vaguely daydreaming 'bout the past in pages of privilege

problem was I unconsciously romanticized dominance and power

with the ultimate vampire not two fanged but a white historian

creating empires in a vacancy by speaking and spreading their own language over many skins like Vaseline

Their mastery of only English is how they gate-keep and stay experts

in their field studying objects that are human beings—

you wanna call that years of experience?

Those YA novels about the utopian — oops I meant the dystopian—

didn't tell me that the barbarians are my politicians and policemen

Superman ain't a Herculean, he an American with money

and an attorney living in the Silicon Valley

I lean in like a willow / running to see the end of the rainbow and grow more

I'm yellow, not mellow, ya can catch me starin' out the window

I got power not from my fucking flower

but as a spider spinning a web of whirlwinds

shooting the lightning before you hear that drop of thunder

Electricity through my veins and diamond in my eyes

Perspectives multifaceted with a soul of gold

Just try to commodify my spirit boy

And I'll rewind back time for you like a toy

Lemme tell ya I'm an avatar because all the mothers that came before me

spoke to me they live and breathe in me

We're connected in our fetal cells

watch me bend syllables upon my will

While you wanna be a firebender look inside that mirror

for the scar hashed out and won't slash in your ego

And then maybe you'll have the growth like Zuko

Still haven't wrote that novel and that's okay because my story is ongoing

the words will keep writing and for now they're in this song spoken into existence

because my voice is resistance

Thank you everyone! This spoken word is my voice as both an Indonesian and Korean woman.

I wrote this piece after 3 mains events:

1. I confided in a friend that I felt like I didn't belong in either Southeast Asian spaces or Korean organizations on UC Berkeley's campus. I explained that in either groups, I felt like an imposter. I had sighed, and told them that I sometimes feel like the equivalent of Panda Express if I were to describe myself as a food. My friend had smiled at me, and told me that there is no such upbringing and lifestyle to represent the Asian/Asian American identity or a specific Asian/Asian American identity. What sticks with me to this day is when she said that my very identities show how the Asian American diaspora has expanded. There is no monolith to speak for the Asian American experience, and having different experiences in upbringing does not make any identity less valid. I now see the dangers in saying "let's put our differences aside" in order to reconcile and work towards a common goal: a future I envision allows differences to exist and does not put forth a singular thought or identity for everyone to agree with.

2. I had recently re-watched Avatar the Last Airbender, and the scene of the Avatar in the Avatar state with all the past Avatars behind him in triangular formation stayed in my mind. When I finally dreamt, I found my being and body was in the Avatar's position, with all my ancestors in triangular formation behind me. I am ready to meet them, learn of them, and become closer to them.

3. I recently read Pramoedya Ananta Toer's *This Earth of Mankind*, which gave me flashbacks to my elementary school that was predominantly white. How desperately I wished to be white,

to be like the popular girls, that I said I wasn't just Indonesian, but lied that I was Dutch Indonesian. How disconnected was I from my mother's history and how much racism did I internalize that I did not understand colonization and imperialism?

For Me

Anh-Vy Phan

Hearts around me are pounding and so is my own. There's a plastic bag, ever so slightly cushioning my knees, but it's not enough. They still hurt. My feet and hands are tingling as chaos erupts around me. A symphony of Zoom calls, video games, and jumbled voices saying "yes!", "no!" "is the midterm…", "too much!", "tomorrow we will…" My pupils are dilating and my palms are growing sweat, and thoughts of uncertainty are rushing to my head.

I want it, but I'm scared.

What if it's not the right time?

But, urgently, a voice in my head whispers,

"But if not now, when?"

My lips are dry and sticky with stale milk tea and grassy jelly residue on them. Riss yanks my ponytail and everyone's eyes fixate on me. I sip my boba more urgently. I don't feel much, just gentle pulling. It's the sound of the scissor that gets me. Every snip breaks a chain.

The reliable daughter.

    The gender dysphoria.

        The doubt.

            The hurt.

                I feel it slowly falling to my feet, poking at my skin as if begging to be let in, but I resist. I refuse.

                Everything becomes more vibrant.

For You

Anh-Vy Phan

Winter is here.

Like the leafless trees,

My head is hairless.

But just as freeing as it feels when shackles are broken,

I, too, am liberated.

I am free from the confines of gender and culture.

My nose has more than two holes.

My ears more than four.

I guess I can smell and hear better.

The winter may be winter, and baby, it may be cold outside, but not here.

Not in my heart. My heart is a growing fire,

My soul is warm,

The source of my serotonin and dopamine is limitless;

It's infinite,

The sky is no longer my ceiling.

I'm here,

I'm me, and I love that.

Nothing can stop me, is that true?

No, nothing can stop me, nothing can hurt me at all…

Nothing but you.

Khong giong ai.

Map nhu heo.

Con co thuong me khong?

Thao cai deo bong muoi ra di con.

Nguang di. Nghe loi me.

Me thuong.

Nhung me thuong ai?

Who do you love?

Who do you hurt?

Am I me?

Or am I who you want me to be?

Am I for you?

Or am I for me?

Who can I be?

Is there a me?

Or is there only you?

Who decides?

Who gets to hurt?

Who gets to cry?

Who do we mourn?

Who has to die?

We Never Left the Boat

Anh-Vy Phan

I'm floating

I'm not in the water

I'm perfectly safe at home

I'm in bed. It feels very firm and stable

The room is so quiet you can hear the rain outside

Pitter patter.

Pitter patter.

I'm fine.

But inside my head? I'm floating

The boat is unstable and the winds are strong

I feel the water splash on my face and stream down from my eyes

It feels so real.

"But, you're in bed. You're safe and free," I tell myself.

"The winds beg to differ. They knock water into the boat.

The sea tugs the boat from side to side

It feels like I'm going to drown.

I close my eyes for second and I see my mom

My grandma

My aunts.

I feel their fair taking over my heart

Holding onto each other, holding onto the boat.

It's cold.

They're scared.

Can't the boat just stabilize?

Can't the ocean just calm?

The boat never stopped rocking

The adrenaline that rushed through their veins is now blood rushing through mine

I can feel it pumping.

Thump, thump.

What a calamity.

The rain is starting to stop now.

It's even quieter than it was before.

I look around my boat and I realize I have something my family didn't.

An anchor.

Perhaps I can try to stop the rocking.

Maybe the ocean won't calm,

But I can try.

Screens

Prinston Pan

The bell rings

Eyelids struggle to open

Rays of the heavens above shine on my face

It is a new day

Unloading Day

Prinston Pan

I vividly remember the tuesdays of my childhood

The old chevrolet express

Dried mud, the dirty shade of white, the creak of the brakes

It slowly backs into the front of the store

The highlight of my week

It was once a week that I felt that I could be of help

The forest green dolly made me feel like superman

I had the strength to transport any box I wanted

Sanctuary

Prinston Pan

Loud shouting, the stench of alcohol, the smoke from cigarettes

Behind that curtain was a different world

It was their safe haven

All night

They refused to leave

It was their only escape from cruel reality

The clack of the hard balls, the thud of it falling in the pocket

The alcohol and smokes the only medicine they had

My hands managed to bleed

Despite the hide its developed through the years

It's no match for the jagged edges of wood

The sharp ends of nails

Or the sparks from the cutting of metal

I guess it's a small price to pay

For the creation of unity

And brighter future for this small town

Where no one is ever alone

Reality

Prinston Pan

Dad was telling me but there was still doubt in my mind

How bad could it be?

That was the main thought in my head

Until I was given a rude awakening

All it took was one email

School was cancelled for the rest of the year

That doubt that has accumulated over months

Vanished within seconds

This was real

It finally arrived

An Unexpected Bond

Prinston Pan

The day I was waiting for

They have finally come for me

To save me

I have been stuck here for some time now

Stuck in the boring oriental store

Days went by slower than ever

Maybe because of anticipation

Maybe because of the uneventfulness

Yet when the day came

My heart dropped

Maybe because of sadness

Maybe because of realization

I had come to grow a certain bond with the store

Despite it being so dull

It became my temporary home

And when I left

I never knew that I would long for those days in the future

Goggles

Prinston Pan

The fading color, the thinning material, the scratched lens

Each trait tells a story, a emotion

The chip on the side lens

A battle scar from my chuck out of frustration

The nose bridge is on its legs

The plastic could snap at anytime

A product of the long nights and the early mornings

The strap has turned from a bright cherry red to a faded, rundown shade

Being constantly soaked in the chlorine and its decaying properties

My goggles tell a story

It has become a part of myself

Preservation

Prinston Pan

The history of my people is beginning to fade

The elders are emotionally scarred

It hurts for them to relive the war

Or think "what would happen if we stayed?"

Yet this is something that our generation must work around

We must realize that we must be wholesome to get to the dark answers we seek

Direct questions will only drag us down

Little steps are the only way

We need to ask questions that bring fond memories

That lead into a deep dark hole

Where the answers are that you seek

The answers that you need to preserve the history of our people

Survived

Prinston Pan

Silence

Hope suffocating

Trusting a stranger to

Seek freedom on the other side.

My life along with my three children

In a whimsy boat on the Mekong River.

Darkness, body awakened by a forceful drag

To dry land. Realization, nobody survived. Heart sank,

Why was I not left to sink to the bottom with my sons.

Freedom has no meaning, freedom is darkness

That is unbearable. Be still my fragile heart.

With calmness comes slow acceptance

Through time. You will always be

In my soul, I will always be

Reminded in the

Eyes of your

New sister.

Love

Offerings to a Silent Mother

Anastasia Doanh Trinh Le

Guilt sounds like organ pipes, an instrument that pairs well with Vietnamese devotional music. On Sunday afternoons, mournful basses and tenors refrain as the sopranos try to reach the limits of their vocal ability without popping off the buttons of their ao dai. The rest of the congregation follows in a comfortable range, which is more a chant inflected by our language's accent than a melody. From above, the organ surrounds us. The pews vibrate, lulling us into a stupor full of unanswerable things: what is the purpose of suffering? Why were people taken from us? How did we all get so far from home? I listen to the priest barrage his intercession in an indiscernible dialect. I learned my prayers in English. Glancing over, I see my mom singing something familiar under her breath, and I wish I knew the words.

Daylight's arc wavers

Knuckles soften like candle wax

Your knowing hands.

A Reflection | Girlhood

Riss Myung

Elementary School

I was never "popular" by conventional standards. I didn't have a friend group to gossip with, people who invited me to share lunches with them, or outfits I would be complimented on. I didn't have the ability to draw in people, make them want to converse with me, and be integrated into groups. I didn't have a large number of friends, period.

It didn't bother me, mostly because I didn't realize I wasn't popular. I was happy with the fact that I consistently had one good friend named Vivian who always invited me to play handball with her during recess after we ate lunch in the cafeteria. After school every Friday, we would go to each other's houses to play together—our moms were close friends in our neighborhood and would cook traditional Chinese dishes together that we eagerly awaited to eat. However, Vivian and her parents moved to China halfway through the school year since her father landed a job there. With this, my little bubble world popped, and I fully realized that I was not popular.

Since then, I floated around friend groups. Most other children were white, with long straight blond hair I was often envious of. They looked like the Barbies my younger sister and I played with in our dollhouse: tall, slim, and Perfect. They got the lead roles in plays and skits, placed in leadership positions, and held the most coveted social positions. Even during recess or PE, no one bothered to aim the ball at them in Dodgeball to get them out—that wasn't supposedly "cool" to do, other than if you were a boy with a crush on one of the girls.

Before we entered class after PE or recess, we had to wait in line outside the door alphabetically according to our last names. The girl in front of me was blonde and tall. I think McKenzie was her name. One day, she turned around and proudly told me that she could wear a "bra," and that she picked it out herself. Then, I didn't know what a "bra" was, so I asked if I could see it.

She started to tug down her shirt, but the boys in front of her must have caught wind of our conversation and turned around, demanding that they show her too. She turned red, crossed her arms, and no longer talked to me.

That day, when my mom picked me up, I asked her what a "bra" was. Once she told me, I felt ashamed that those boys must have known what that article of clothing was before I did. I felt even more ashamed that I had embarrassed the girl in front of me. But most of all, I felt ashamed that my breasts had not developed then. I wasn't aware that bodies developed at different rates. So I felt different and thought there was something wrong with me. These were conversations I never had with anyone in my family, and the subject matter didn't re-open till middle school.

Middle School

In my science class, there was a curriculum called "Family Life," where teachers introduce children to the anatomy of our bodies, or more specifically, our reproductive parts. Towards the end of the concepts, the teachers showed a video of a mother giving birth and walked us methodologically through how a woman became pregnant. Female teachers taught female students, and male teachers taught male students.

To this day, I don't remember much about what we learned. I know we labelled parts of the vagina, but it never felt like we were talking about body parts that were on my own body. Instead, I remember the giggles of the girls excited to be solely around their girlfriends in one class, and the boys complaining that they wanted to be in the girls' class too. The girls with boyfriends took and sent pictures of the worksheets, depicting the anatomy of the vagina, to them. Those without boyfriends mostly texted each other from across the classroom.

I remember sitting in the back of the classroom. I didn't have a phone (and wouldn't have a phone until my sophomore year in high school) so I didn't have anyone to text. I learned that if I had my head down, my fingers skimming the paper handout, the teacher never called me, thinking that I was working. Plus, she always tended to call on the girls on their phones, so I was safe.

However, the classroom itself wasn't a safe space where I felt comfortable asking questions about my own body parts. I knew that my body didn't develop as fast as others, but I didn't want to ask *why* in the classroom and embarrass myself. Yet, such was inevitable. In one of the discussions, there came a point where bra size came up. While I (thankfully) knew what a bra was, I didn't know my size. So when the girls in the row in front of me turned around and asked what bra size I was, I merely responded that I forgot. One turned towards the other and snickered that I probably couldn't fit into a bra.

The truth was, I didn't own a regular bra. I only wore sports bras so when I ran club cross country or track afterwards, I wouldn't have to fully change. Plus, regular bras were extremely expensive, and it wasn't until later in high school did I wear my mother's hand me downs and own an 'actual' bra.

Another point came up about periods, and how long our ovulation cycles normally last. I hadn't had my period yet (and wouldn't have my period till high school). Because nearly every girl had had their period in the room, they talked about their experiences for the first time bleeding. The earlier the date occurred, the more confidence seemed to brim from them. Before they turned their attention towards me, I asked the teacher to be excused to the bathroom.

In "Family Life," yes we did learn about our reproductive parts. But I also learned that my body was 'behind' in terms of development. I wasn't even sure why the curriculum was called "Family Life" itself. Did actions related to sex serve as the fundamental basis of a family structure? I wasn't sure. I didn't learn about other family life-styles outside my own and my parent's friends until high school. Until then, I felt lost and confused and ashamed of and in my body.

High School

The first time I visited one of my best friend's houses in high school, I was shocked. Open windows and pulled up blinds so that the sunlight spilled in, crayons and colored pencils sprawled lazily across a table, my friend's youngest sibling dancing around the kitchen and singing a song for her school play, and colorful cups scattered across the main table. Outside in the backyard, a makeshift hammock swung slightly from the breeze, stirring up crisp leaves on the ground.

It was open and beautiful. Mesmerizing.

It made me think of Sula's house in Toni Morrison's novel, and I told my friend's mom that. Then our conversation shifted to how the education system was meant to fail those who couldn't afford higher education from the start, and how the income gap between the top ten percent and those below the poverty line is unbelievable. I've never had these conversations with an adult before other than my teachers—and it's even harder for me to perceive my teachers outside the classroom as regular people.

I've grown up modeling adults in the workforce as professionals who reached their zenith across all facets of life, so having open discussions with them to me seemed to question their authority. After all, the slightest bit of disagreement in my household warranted punishment. Talking back, saying no, or simply setting boundaries was seen as a sign of disrespect in my family.

Thus, I was amazed that my friend could talk to her mother and father about her exes and current boyfriend. How he kissed her, how she met his parents, and so on and so forth. On the other hand, my mother didn't meet my father's parents until the day of the wedding.

Of course, times are changing. Sometimes I feel as if my parent's cultural values have caused my upbringing to precede slower compared to others, like a rusted cog on one of the wheels of mainstream society plowing forward. I didn't realize that Difference was something to be celebrated until college. I didn't realize that the public educational system taught science, or more specifically biology, on a standard scale that mostly pertained to majority populations. I didn't realize that my body didn't develop necessarily slower, but average according to my mother, and my mother's mother. I didn't realize the importance of history passed down onto me and living within me today. I didn't realize the dangers of a single story being taught within a larger framework.

College

In retrospect, I wish that I had other friends that looked like me in elementary school so I wouldn't have been aware of my Difference. I wish there was a mental health equivalent to the "Family Life" course in middle school so that I had the resources to deal with my emerging eating disorder stemming from body insecurity and body dysmorphia. I wished that I felt comfortable casually conversing with my parents in high school so that I could feel at ease within my own home.

Attending a University of California, with a large population of students from all walks of life, I've met people with bits of pieces of myself in them, and different parts as well. Some students have also never heard their parents truly say, "I love you," and if so, only on rare occasions. Some students don't live with their parents for a variety of reasons. Some female-identifying students choose not to wear a bra, and walk around confidently in their bodies. It is these testimonies and voices and representation that I lacked growing up.

I've asked my friends what sexual slang meant. They've told me the definitions, and also that they thought it was 'cute' and 'pure' that I didn't know what blue balls meant. I wonder if I was in elementary school now if my peers would think that me not knowing what a bra was, was 'cute.' Of course, searching for a definitive answer would prove futile, but to walk across a campus where our upbringings have played a vital role in shaping our lives, I can't help but think, what if I didn't grow up in an Asian household?

Would I have been popular? Would there not have been a stigma talking about our bodies and reproduction? Would I be able to hold a casual conversation with my parents about my day? Would

I be able to hug my parents without feeling a sense of aversion? Would I be able to tell my parents I love them?

If I was more immersed with either of my parent's cultural roots, then would I have been popular with people who looked like me? If I could speak Korean or Indonesian, would I have been treated differently? Who am I, a reflection of who, and which culture, exactly?

—problems with having a body born in America but does not feel American, and knowing that your body is not home to your cultures within a standardized system

Filipino Talk Stories

Alyssa Ranola

My mom's hometown in Lucena City.

A couple of weeks ago, I was standing in the stairwell talking to my cousin. He was pestering me about why I broke up with my boyfriend. He had been drinking at my uncle's house pretty nearby. The last time we had hung out together, I had been sad and was drinking. It was boy problems, a myopic but age-old issue. Today he had just popped in to visit and started asking where my boyfriend was – in the Philippines, you drink with the boys, not the girls, so it only made sense (despite how wildly sexist that would be here in America). I told him we had broken up. Thus began the questions.

I knew my cousin and I thought very differently about love and relationships. I eventually pried myself open and told him that I didn't want to take care of my boyfriend forever, that I was tired, and if I didn't stand up for myself I would be caring for him always. My cousin was disappointed in the answer.

"So if you get another boyfriend, are you just going to leave?" he asked.

I didn't know. He had a point. The hardwood floors my dad had made were cold under my feet and I felt a bit tired. It was 2, maybe 3 in the morning. My cousin leaned against the wall, waiting for me to answer as opposed to sitting on the comfortable couch in the living room 10 feet away.

"I don't need another guy. I can be happy by myself," I said. I briefly wondered if my parents or my brother could hear our conversation upstairs. My uncle lay snoring on the couch already, waiting for his son to accompany his lonely slumber.

"So you're gonna be alone forever?" he said.

"I don't care, I can just be there for me."

"Stop it," he said. "Don't copy me. I'm alone because I thought that way."

That gave me pause. He seemed miserable. For whatever reason, he would always come whenever he wanted to drink and was sort of infamous to my dad for being a mischief-maker these days.

My cousin and I transitioned to sit on the floor. It was cold. My cousin had a blanket that he had drawn around him, tightly. He laughed from how cold he was.

Then as we talked, he started to transition to different reasons as to his lull in mood. He said that the church only cares about money, because in the Quezon province my uncle was from, when my cousin's mother passed away and his grandpa around the same time, the church wouldn't accept his mom to be buried there because she wasn't married. I had never met my cousin's mom, but remembered her framed picture in our living room when my cousins still visited frequently. She was beautiful with black hair and eyes that smiled when she smiled. I remembered how hit with grief all 3 of my cousins were the day that she passed, how they went from laughing and joking with my parents and our uncles and aunts to shutting up like trap doors, their faces hard as stone. The whole house felt empty and deserted.

My cousin was bitter. His objection was a pretty forbidden view to hold about the church from a first-generation son who grew up fully indoctrinated in strong, Catholic beliefs in God. The church he talked about was a really big, fancy one right smack in the middle of the town of Lucban, which "had a lot of history" so I had heard from the priest when I had visited. It was pretty Gothic looking from the outside – exposed to the elements and all that. From the inside it was just as ancient, suffused with the reverence and peace of prayers, candles lit by stray wanderers, people coming just to pray to the large statues of Jesus under the echoing, looming ceilings. Probably if any place in Quezon was holy, that place was.

But did my cousin not have the right to have his mom in the church cemetery? It was the same cemetery my own grandpa had been taken to after his passing. My cousin's mom should have had the same benefit.

He said that around the time of both his grandpa and mother's passing, he was very depressed. He said that he can't be close to people anymore, just in case. That everyone moves on – once you die, friends, even family forget about you.

That triggered me. My mom and dad would care if I died. When my family had faced significant and seemingly insurmountable challenges in recent years, my parents hunkered down like nobody's business for their children. Our family would have to be nuked for my parents to stop caring, whether I or my brother liked it or not. Nuked to smithereens, to dust, to atomic particles.

"Not family," I said. "My mom and dad wouldn't forget about me."

My cousin insisted. Even family, after a long enough time, will forget about you. He spoke about his older brothers and how they moved on after his family's passing. How as the youngest, he has to be alone since his brothers both have their own lives.

After a while, he said he was too cold, and I urged us to move to the couch. Then my cousin trailed off onto other topics until he fell asleep.

My mother looking over the horizon.

My parents both immigrated from the Philippines around 1996 and met shortly after establishing stable work. My mom had come following my grandma and her siblings to America. My grandma had been working in nursing homes all over, caretaking for older women in Washington and then in the US. My mom's large family was making moves in a variety of ways, with my aunt's husband working for the military, and my uncle working in the nursing home. Most of my family worked in health care: cue the stereotype about the abundance of Filipino nurses.

It was hard to think about my grandma bustling about, taking care of 9 other children from my mom and then moving to America to make money that she would send back to support them from afar. My grandma, who we and most all of the extended Ranola family called Nanay (Mom in Tagalog), would babysit my brother and I with my grandpa when we were kids. She made us suman, nilaga, and adobo every day, and then turned around and hoarded bags and boxes piled to the ceiling in her room. Then after school she would come by bus to walk me home from school, a huge smile on her face as we crunched our sneakers down the gravelly street with wide brimmed hats keeping out the sun.

While my mother's family had a complicated story with many players, my dad's was somewhat more subtle. All I knew was that my dad had come with his parents and one other sister. My family would go to the Philippines every other year to visit my mom's family, and that my Nanay and Tatay who made us suman and walked me home were from my mom's side as well. While I felt like every part of my body was a Ranola, this whole other side to my family, Dela Cruz, was hidden under unsaid words and shadows of people instrumental to my dad's upbringing. Of my dad, I knew tales told only when my dad was drunk, about walking miles through dark, haunted woods to get to school and a friend with no legs up to the knee, who could swim so well, to my dad he was the "Human Fish." I of course also knew that my dad was a technician and had worked at hotels before his current job fixing parts at restaurants.

Even in the family dynamic, this silence on my dad's part was represented. Whatever my mom said went, whether we would get Thai food before going to my brother's graduation, or whether or not I could go on a sleepover, or whether we were going to church. My dad would quietly wait through the service, serving family time rather than my mom's holy time.

Still, my dad loved my brother and I deeply. I still recall the ways he would tease me and play with me as I grew up, taking me to the library, the park, my cousins' house in American Canyon (perhaps the only family on his side we were remotely close to), and calling me "little girl" with a playful tone. He even advised me when a boy picked a fight with me in elementary school, telling me to fake-cry (ending in the boy losing badly and limping off the field, a shameful moment on my part.)

My mom and dad came from vastly different areas and were even different ages with a 10 year age gap. But they saw enough in each other to stick together for 20 years.

As a second-generation kid of Filipino immigrants, I encounter a lot of cultural clashings or interminglings between my American and Filipino roots. This one day is when I learned more about the talk stories that my family passes down to me, and the way that I can feel so small and swamped in history in a single family out of the millions in America. It is the root of my narcissism, that my parents love me intensely, and that they have a fiery passion for our success, from all that they have sacrificed to give to me. It is also the root of my insecurity where I will never be enough to sate a hunger for safety and stability running deeper than bone for over my 23 years, as every generation passes the desperate resilience to me, in silence brimming with listless and watchful waiting.

Earlier the same night I had spoken to my cousin, I was sitting at the table when my dad came in at around midnight. He seemed happy after drinking at my uncle's house.

I had 2 burgers on the table from going to In N Out. My brother was sleeping on the couch.

"Whose burger is this?" my dad said.

"It's nobody's. Take it," I said. I had bought an extra just in case anyone wanted it.

"Christian, there's a burger!" my dad said.

"It's okay dad, you can eat it," I said. I was partway through my own burger.

"Are you sure?" he asked. He was eating some of the fries. Eventually, I convinced him my brother wasn't going to be getting up and told him to have some of his burger.

"But then I'm gonna be too full," he said. My dad had gotten into the habit of not eating full, regular meals, despite working hard manual labor for a job. My dad is a technician. He may not always be working with heavy ass cars the way he does as a hobby, but the way that he comes home and sneaks away to the back with a couple of beers somehow showed his exhaustion clear as day.

In the past month or so, my dad had maintained a slim physique, but I worried as this was not a healthy nutrition plan. It was unreasonable for him to work himself to the bone when it was unnecessary, when he could work himself to the average BMI instead and retain some comfort. He acted as though it was not too hard a loss.

"Ate, if I quit my job, will you help me?" he asked. Ate was the word for sister in Tagalog, which my brother called me often. It was a nickname, kind of. More like an honorific that my parents used often to encourage my brother.

"What?"

"Will you help me?"

Panic rose inside me. "With what? With groceries? With bills?"

My dad laughed. "Everything. Will you help me."

I was confused. He was drunk, though, and I didn't really know what he meant. I ate more of my In N Out burger. It was an ordinary cheeseburger, which was all I was comfortable with. I never got the double double that my brother was fond of.

"Work is getting stressful."

"What happened?" I asked.

"There was this new guy. And you know, I have an accent. 'Label,' you know what that is?"

"Label?" I thought he meant on a bottle.

"See, you don't understand me even. Label."

Eventually, I realized.

"Level," I said.

"Yeah! Level," my dad said. My dad probably needed the level to install machinery properly, and a new guy, more of a novice than himself who had worked at the company for 10 years and risked his other job to work there, had the nerve to challenge his accent. "He couldn't understand me. It made me so pissed off. He was so rude."

I was confused. I had just done the same thing that this stranger had done to my dad. My dad didn't seem angry at me. I guessed it was about the specifics of the situation though.

"Is there anything else that has been stressing you out?"

My dad explained that there had been a lot of work lately since the pandemic started. He said that the driver wasn't going to transport some oil container because it wasn't his job anymore. My dad couldn't tell his manager about it, but rather had to transport the thing himself and install it alone. It seemed like people weren't communicating about the changes in workload, and my dad was doing things out of his job description.

"I'm sorry dad," I said.

"It's okay." He looked at me. "I just want you to be successful."

I suddenly became desperate, generations of tryhards bleeding through my jittery, 1 am skin. "Yeah, well, I'm going to be a substitute soon."

He perked up.

"Once I submit all the documents I can be an emergency substitute. And that's a real job. I'm going to get an actual salary and everything. It's enough to live off of." I supposed. I wasn't going to be a full-time substitute, though.

"That's great!" my dad said. "Is there anything else you're interested in?"

"Yes, there's this networking event I'm going to next week. It's for publishing. I'm really hoping I can learn a lot more about publishing and everything through it." I know, I was desperate, but my entire mindset was aimed for professional progress those last weeks. The networking session was really close to an important grad school interview and I just wanted the answers. My anxiety about my future stewed in my mind with my worthlessness as a daughter. To be Asian was to be a tryhard, to play catch-up with other minorities; it seemed stamped into my brain from movies and books. The model minority pressure exerted on me my entire life came to the forefront: the way that Asians are made to compete and win, according to the dominant narrative. I had to fulfill the expectation of me that the whole world had, but more importantly, that my parents had.

"Great!" My dad smiled widely. He looked radiantly happy. Proud. "I just want you to be successful," he said again. "You don't have to do anything else. Just work on becoming successful."

My dad continued, eating the burger. I told him to finish it because he hadn't eaten all day, despite his protestations about getting too full. It was then that he began to talk about his experience immigrating from the Philippines to America.

He said he was the youngest out of 8 or so brothers and sisters. He had 2 sisters, one in America and one elder sister still in the Philippines. He had a handful of brothers, one of whom had had a million pesos, others who had stayed in the Philippines to start their own lives.

He said that he had gone to Manila to do tricycle work to make a living since he had left high school. His parents were doing paperwork to immigrate to America. His brother came to his place in Manila and told him to come home because his parents had something to tell him.

He said he came home, in Pangasinan, another island off from Manila, and an over 8-hour drive. He knocked on the door so hard that it fell down, off of its hinges, flat onto the floor. He asked his parents. They said, "We're going to America. You're coming with us."

It had never been his intention to head to America. Still, it was the day that his whole life changed. A day marked with insurmountable importance, where his life was divided into "before" and "after."

He went to America. Many of his older siblings stayed, and have stayed there their whole lives. It was only himself, his sister, and his parents because he had been the youngest and so had the luck of going.

I asked him more about his siblings, particularly his older sister, who I had never met. I asked why we hadn't gone to see her.

"I tried to go see her," he said. "I told your mom we should go see her. She passed away."

This was news to me. I asked him when she passed away.

He got very quiet. "A month or so after we left the Philippines."

I was shocked, but not surprised. My dad kept his emotions under lock and key, and as Asian Americans there was a culture of secrecy surrounding suffering and negative emotions. To let others know that we were in pain was to open ourselves up to scrutiny that was looked down on in Filipino culture. "Hiya" dictated that if you were different from everybody else, you deserved the shame that would surely follow. "Pakikisama" is the idea that you need to follow the crowd so that no one feels uncomfortable and relationships are smooth.

Even though I was not surprised, I told him I was sorry. I told him I wished we could have seen her. He said that mom's siblings, my aunts and uncles, had said that they didn't want to go, and mom told him that we couldn't go, so we didn't end up taking the detour to see his sister who lived nearby. Whenever we went to the Philippines, we would all take a van and ride together to wherever we needed to go. This made sense because we would often do activities around Manila and then go to Quezon province, where my grandma and my mom had lived before, which was a 5 or so hour drive away. It made sense also how my quiet dad, who didn't want to get in anyone's way or spit on anyone's welcome, would not want to force my aunts and uncles' hand, not knowing that his sister would have passed away.

My dad ended up going to bed soon after that, as a night of drinking usually made him sleepy, as it does anyone. I stayed up, stunned into stillness, unknowingly waiting for my cousin to start a similar conversation.

These stories, though especially my dad's about the door falling down and all his siblings speaking to him about it, are replicated in many immigrants' lives. Second-generation children become accustomed to the back and forth of their many cultures intersecting. Eating Filipino food, speaking English and Tagalog – it becomes commonplace, as basic as the fact that the sun rises and sets every day. Yet it comes down to these significant days. We don't know, because we don't ask. But if it were not for those days in our parents lives where they were taken aside and told to go to America, when they made that pivotal decision, where would they be now? Would my dad still be driving a tricycle around Manila? Would my mom be finishing her education to become a nurse instead of making company calls all day for work?

My dad and cousin's stories further engage the question of what does it mean for a person to immigrate from one country to another? From the Philippines, where everything is humid and hot, where you can walk up to a stranger and ask for a cigarette and neighbors are as good as family, to the United States, where you have to pump gas yourself, and in some cities, nobody would help if you were hit or stabbed? Even details down to the plants are different: tamed in orderly squares by sidewalks or in the islands on roads, versus bushes and vibrant flowers crawling over properties, trees and plants towering and large lizards crawling like you live in a forest with a city in it rather than the other way around. How do you go to sleep at night and not dream you are home, at your real home, and not wake up confused and hurt some days, or grateful, or lonely? What does it mean to go to work and just miss family with your whole heart and soul, only to not communicate that to people, how you just feel like you want to touch plants that close on their own, or want to hug your brother or visit your mom?

My cousin's story hits very close to home. As someone straddling 2 cultures that perceive religion very differently, I have been struggling myself. On the one hand, the Philippines believes strongly in God and in the afterlife. While some Filipinos are Muslim or one of the various other Christian denominations, a majority are Catholic. In America, particularly in liberal California, most people my age – early to late 20s – are atheist, and being Christian is the minority. You are mocked for it most times, if not to your face, then behind your back. How could you support a religion which is the cause of child abuse and murder? Columbus day is still a holiday despite his mass murders of Native Americans, and he came preaching about Christianity. Filipinos are Catholic because the Spaniards who colonized were Catholic, and I doubt that colonizers came with warm hugs.

Still, I know 2 very different narratives about Christianity. But the arguments against it are irrelevant to the fact that a woman who deserved to be buried in a decent church was not buried there simply because she was not married. If we went condemning and punishing people based on their sins, the world would be on fire. We would be in chaos. It makes no sense to punish a person for not marrying. Furthermore, my cousin is now in America, worlds away from where his mother is buried. How does that feel, to be oceans away from your own mom, and to not even have in confidence the fact that she is buried somewhere spiritually secure, in the city she called home? There is so much wrong with all of this. If you are going to hurt people senselessly with unbelievable standards, there is no point to your morals about God. If your standards are so high that they demolish people, what kind of faith do you have? Do you really believe that slinging hateful words and laws will somehow bring peace? Having hoops for people to jump through so that you are happy with them makes no sense and begets more pain than understanding and togetherness. Obedience to God becomes a sick joke when you pair it with senseless rules like, "You must be married to have children." Aren't we supposed to turn the other cheek? What example is the church setting?

There is so much trauma mixed into immigrating from another place to a new place. Immigration and trauma go hand in hand with no way to neatly divide them. Just like my Filipino American identity, we will never be able to reconcile these differences and the pain and happiness either experience brings. All we can do is acknowledge it, talk about it, and slowly begin to heal.

Me and my dad.

Simon - Wrong Destiny

Phibi Tran

Chapter 1: Promises

"Britney, hurry! There isn't much time!"

"Simon, it's still a prototype! And I don't even know if it'll work!"

"Just do it already! If I can go back to the past, I can fix things before it's too late."

"I don't want to lose my one and only brother!" Britney cried.

"I'll be okay. I'll come back soon. I promise."

Britney activates the prototype of her time machine. Simon's body shakes and he loses consciousness and breath.

As the smell of sầu riêng fills the room, Britney cries "Simon! No!"

~ ~

Simon, although barely conscious, hears a mysterious voice call out, "chữa được bệnh, không ái chữa được mệnh."

Suddenly Simon is surrounded by an ocean and calls out, "Britney..." before he fully submerges into the water around him.

~ ~

"Britney!" Simon screams as he wakes up in his bed. "What?"

Simon looks around and it seems that nothing has changed. Although he feels different. He looks into the mirror and is surprised by his younger reflection staring back at him.

"Wow I feel like I'm 18 again. I guess the machine did work after all. I've got to tell Britney!"

Simon checks his phone to try to contact Britney, but there is no trace of her existence anywhere. "What? Britney?"

He feels his phone vibrate in his pocket and he gets a text message from an unknown sender. He opens the text only for it to appear as indecipherable gibberish that suddenly transformed into a message he could read.

"Simon, if you're reading this, that means that my machine worked. I don't even know if this will even reach you or if you can even reply. I have attached the blueprints for my machine in this text. Please come back to me. Love, Britney."

~ ~

"Hey mẹ whatever happened to ông nội?" asked the first of the three grandsons.

"Con, you wouldn't understand. I never knew my dad. He died when I was young," replied the anxious mother.

"Well what was his name?" inquired the second grandson.

"Simon was his name. I'll tell you the story about him when you get older. Don't worry too much about him. Just focus on the present, here and now."

"Okay thanks mẹ," smiled the third grandson. The three grandchildren looked at each other and smiled. They later went up to the attic where they would discover a photograph of Simon as well as his biography. In the past, he was a heavily persecuted grassroots community organizer who fought for the liberation. According to his older sister, he had died from a freak accident. After his death, his comrades succeeded in creating a liberated world that abolished the systems of oppression and brought about prosperity among humanity.

"Bác Britney!"

"What are you kids doing snooping around here? Is that… Simon?" asked Aunt Britney intently staring at Simon's photograph.

"We just got curious and wanted to know more about ông nội," the grandsons murmured.

"Does cháu Thúy know you're here? You read about my prototype didn't you?"

"Did Simon actually die?"

"I don't know. I sent Simon a message and although he promised me that he would come back, he never did. And so over the past few decades, I've devoted my life to improving my machine in order to bring him back," sighed Aunt Britney.

"We want to help! Let us bring Simon back!" the grandsons excitedly yelled.

~ ~

"Hey Simon, I think we're ready to test out your prototype. I've never seen anything like it before!" exclaimed Thuận, Simon's cognitive science colleague in graduate school.

"I never thought this day would come. My older sister actually passed on this blueprint to me and I added my own twist to it. With this machine, I should be able to contact my grandparents who fled Việt Nam after the Fall of Sài Gòn in 1975. I want to ask them more about what their lives were like."

"Simon, you don't even speak Vietnamese. How are you even going to talk to them?"

"Tao biết… nói Tiếng Việt được… mà!"

"Mày luôn ngu như con bò."

"Cảm ơn bạn. Okay, let's set up the machine!"

Simon sat into the chair of the machine. Thuận attached the machine's helmet to Simon's head and pricked Simon's finger to get a sample of blood to put into the machine's vials.

"Can't you be more gentle Thuận?"

"Using your blood is the only way we can connect with your bloodline. Besides, you invented this machine yourself so you should know what's going to happen."

"Just remember to put a band-aid on it afterward. Let's begin!"

Thuận started the machine and the blood sample suddenly disappeared from the vials. Simon's eyes started to rapidly move as if he was in REM sleep. Simon started to murmur something unintelligible in Vietnamese. Thuận got worried and started to double check Simon's vitals. Everything seemed to be in order.

~ ~

"Anh ơi! Anh có thấy con bươm bướm đó không?" yelled Xuân.

"Em thấy cái gì? Con bươm bướm?" wondered Lộc.

"Chào ông nội! Chào bà nội!" exclaimed Simon.

"Ủa? Mày là ai? Về quê đi!" screamed Xuân.

"Mày là ma hả? Mày muốn chết hả?" Lộc threatened.

"I swear I'm not a ghost! My name is Simon and I'm from the future! Please don't hurt me!" pleaded Simon as he morphed from his butterfly form into his human form.

"Really now? What do you want? So you're our grandson?" Xuân inquired.

"You still look as ugly as a ghost," Lộc mocked.

"I came because I wanted to learn more about my family history. I don't speak Vietnamese that well and you two had died before I had the chance to ask you. Wait, how can you understand me right now? I thought you two don't speak any English," Simon looked at them with a puzzled expression.

"We don't speak English. But yet, we can still talk to you somehow. We're not even awake right now. We're still in our dreams," answered Lộc.

"Ah, it must be through the power of your love. This type of magic runs through our blood. Love has no language barriers. Ask us anything con," Xuân lovingly replied.

Unsure of how long he had in the dream world, Simon asked as many questions as he could and learned a lot about his family history. He had learned about the history of the colonization of Việt Nam as well as the imperialist forces that led to Lộc.and Xuân fleeing to the United States. It felt as if they were talking for an eternity. Eventually, Lộc and Xuân were beginning to wake up and fade away.

"Wait! There's still more I need to know!" Simon yelled pointlessly. Suddenly, he heard the sound of three children's voices.

"Uống nước," sang the first grandson.

"nhớ nguồn," sang the second grandson.

"ăn quả," sang the third grandson.

"nhớ kẻ trồng cây!" sang all three grandsons in unison.

Simon looked behind him and saw three small children running up to him.

"Simon!" they cried as they surrounded him with a warm hug.

"Who are you little ones? And why aren't you all in the shape of a butterfly? And what were you kids even saying?"

"Bác Britney sent us! We've come to save you! She said that if we keep chanting that phrase, it'll make sure we never forget where we came from. It means when you drink water, remember the source. And when you eat fruit, remember the one who planted the tree."

"Britney…"

A loud voice echoed through the space-time continuum they were in. "chữa được bệnh, không ái chữa được mệnh."

Suddenly, Simon and the three grandsons began to sink into the ground as if they were being enveloped by quicksand.

Chapter 2: Returning

"I don't have much time left," lamented Britney.

"We know Bác Britney! It took us a long time, but we've finally repaired your time machine! I think we can go back and save Simon now!" exclaimed the three grandsons, now several years older.

"Simon…" Bác Britney sighed

"Your health is getting worse, Bác Britney," the grandsons worried.

"We only have one shot to do this. Let's go guys! Bác Britney, please push this button when we tell you to!" the three grandsons yelled in excitement.

The three grandsons had repaired Bác Britney's time machine and tweaked it so they could fully travel to the past, but they could not return unless they could build a time machine back to the future. After setting up the machine, the third grandson strapped himself into the chair and told Bác Britney to push the button. The grandsons slowly faded as they sank into the ground, returning back to the land.

~ ~

"Simon? Hello? Simon! You're awake!"

"Thuận… is everything okay?"

"You had me scared back there. You started violently shaking and I didn't know what to do! All of your vitals started to drop and it looked as if you had fully lost consciousness and became brain dead, yet you were still breathing somehow."

"Really. Wow. My head hurts for some reason. All I can last remember is hearing three voices. I don't know what happened back there, but I'm glad to have made it out okay. I'm going to go home and rest now."

"Slow down there! Let me drive you back home. You almost lost balance there!"

~ ~

The next day Simon woke up in his bed and nothing seemed out of the ordinary until he looked around and saw three figures staring at him.

"Uhhh, hello? Who are you and what are you doing here?" Simon cautiously asked.

"Simon, it's us! Don't you remember when we hugged you? Granted we were kids back then," the first grandson replied.

"But it's only been a day. How can you have possibly grown up so fast? I don't even know your names!" Simon says in shock.

The three grandsons tell Simon their names, but Simon's Vietnamese isn't good enough to understand, so he decides to call them P, L, and T respectively.

"Several years have gone by for us, Simon. Bác Britney has aged now and she doesn't have that many years left in her," mourned P.

"Chị Britney…" Simon lamented. "I have to hurry and get back to her immediately before it's too late!"

"Simon, we have bad news. The time machine Bác Britney invented has never been able to travel to the future. She said you cannot go to a future that doesn't exist yet. In fact, we came here on a one-way trip to help you build a time machine that can go to the future. She gave us the blueprint," L informed.

Simon carefully looks at the blueprint. "This isn't possible. We currently don't have the technology or resources to make anything this advanced."

"What do you mean? Just simply ask your government to help fund it. At least that's what we did in our timeline," T scoffs.

"In this timeline, we live in a capitalist society. There's no way I can even get the clearance nor the funding for this. Even repairing my current machine would be costly as it is," Simon remarks.

Simon's phone vibrates and he realizes it's a text from chị Britney.

"Simon. This message should reach you soon. By now, you should have met your grandsons again. I did some research on your timeline and in your timeline, I have already died. And my heart is the key. I also learned that my name isn't actually Britney. It's Bươm Bướm."

Chapter 3: Remembering

"I hope my nephews are okay. Even if they do find Simon again, there's no guarantee that they'll be able to make it all back here safely. I need to help them. I can still send Simon one last text," Britney thought to herself. As Britney does research on Simon's timeline, she starts to question why her grandparents even came to America in the first place. She never got the chance to learn about their family history. Although she now lives in a liberated world, she hates the fact that people had to fight for it. She wonders what life would even be like if imperialist America never entered the Vietnam War or even bombed Southeast Asia. As she does more research and learns the truth about her name and her death in Simon's timeline, Bươm Bướm starts to shake and have a panic attack as her heart rate rapidly increases. She enters an existential crisis about her existence as Britney. Her real name had been Bươm Bướm this whole time and her parents never told her.

~ ~

"Hey Simon, I did some research on Bác Bươm Bướm and apparently in this timeline, she had died in Sài Gòn, which is now known as Hồ Chí Minh City. There is an urban legend that four distinct butterflies have been known to hover in circles over her grave from time to time. And she cannot fully rest until the butterflies make their way back to her. Until then, the butterflies are stuck in an endless cycle of life and death. It is tradition to make offers of hoa mai to her grave to help guide the butterflies to her. Otherwise, she will haunt anyone who visits her grave," explained P.

"Didn't Bác Bươm Bướm say that her heart was the key? I bet that if we dig up her and take her heart out to use in our time machine, her blood should be able to connect us back to her so we can return to the future!" frantically yelled L.

"That's a horrible idea and disrespectful to her too," T scolded.

"That's ridiculous. When she said 'my heart is the key,' she meant her lover. Before I came to this timeline, I remember Britney, I mean Bươm Bướm, telling me that she was in love with this one girl. I think her name was 'Lily!'" Simon's eyes lit up as he recalled.

"There's no records of anyone named Lily. However, in this universe, 'Lily' is actually 'Chanh,' Bác Bươm Bướm's secret lover!" P exclaimed!

Simon and PLT immediately booked a flight to Hồ Chí Minh City, Việt Nam to visit Bươm Bướm's grave for clues and find Chanh.

~ ~

Simon and PLT made it safely to Hồ Chí Minh City and were on their way to Bươm Bướm's grave.

"Hey Simon. When you used your time machine, you were able to go back in time and talk to your grandparents in your dreams. Since you were able to ask them about your family history, I think it's fair now that we're here to ask about yours!" P laughed.

"As you know, I went back and met my paternal grandfather, Lộc and my paternal grandmother, Xuân. They had a son named Việt, who married a nice woman named Kiều. They then had me, Simon, and my sister Britney, who is actually Bươm Bướm."

"Simon, do you have a Vietnamese name?" inquired L.

"The story is that both of my parents weren't that good at Vietnamese and they barely spoke it. They called themselves 'byelingual' as a joke. They named me Simon and tried to convert it into a Vietnamese name by giving me the name 'Sai mệnh.' I still don't know what it means, but I think it sounds cool!" Simon replied.

"Your name means wrong destiny. And it's not even grammatically correct. It's supposed to be 'mệnh sai,'" snickered T.

"Dang it, Mom and Dad!" Simon cursed in frustration, "Anyways we've basically arrived."

Upon reaching the grave site, they saw four butterflies hovering in a circle around Bươm Bướm's grave. An unknown woman wearing a full black áo dài kneeled down to place hoa mai on

Bươm Bướm's grave and then started to cry. After wiping her tears, she got up and looked directly at Simon.

"I know why you are here. I didn't expect this day to come so soon." Chanh hands Simon a butterfly pin that has its wings replaced as lemons. "You'll need this to save Bươm Bướm. Save her for me."

Simon and PLT were incredibly confused by what just happened. "Chanh, thank you."

"There's no time. Just go! You can thank me later," Chanh yelled and ran off.

Chapter 4: Destiny

"This is it guys. After building a new time machine and with this final piece, the lemon butterfly pin, we'll finally be able to travel back to the future and reunite with Bươm Bướm!" Simon said with excitement.

"That was actually pretty smart of her to use that pin to capture and preserve her blood! It should still work just fine!" P remarked.

"Did you guys get water on the blueprint? For some reason there's a part here that got smudged but it's still readable," L asked.

"One of you gúy must have dropped it or something back when we were in Việt Nam. It should be fine," T chuckled.

Simon and PLT prepared the time machine and loaded up the blood. Simon and PLT faded and rose into the sky. Suddenly, they were surrounded by an ocean of water. Boats started to move towards and encase them into a wooden cocoon. They were ready to fly into the future. Their wooden cocoons suddenly hatched and they grew beautiful butterfly wings as soft as handwoven silk fabric. They started flying towards a vision of Bươm Bướm when suddenly their wings were cut off. A mysterious voice said, "chữa được bệnh, không ái chữa được mệnh." They fell down to the ground of the space-time continuum and sank into the ground just like last time.

Simon wakes up in an unfamiliar bedroom. He smells bánh xèo from downstairs and hears the sound of several mô tô outside. As expected, PLT were staring at him. Yet something was different. They started speaking to him purely in Vietnamese and he was able to understand it fully as if he was a fluent speaker. He realized that he could finally understand what their names P, L, and T, meant.

"A lô? Simon có ở đây không? Simon có nghè cháu được không?" Phước asked.

"Ủa? Simon hiểu chúng ta được!" Lộc exclaimed.

"Giỏi quá!" Thọ joked.

"Woah, I can finally understand you guys now. I don't even need to speak English anymore!" Simon happily replied in Vietnamese. "Come on, let's go downstairs and eat! It smells amazing!"

"Sai mệnh. Something's wrong. While you were unconscious, we were able to do some research on this timeline. Apparently we never made it back to the future. We seem to be in the past, but in a timeline where America never entered Southeast Asia. Your grandparents never fled South Việt Nam during the Fall of Sài Gòn in 1975. We're in a completely alternate universe," Phước stated in Vietnamese.

"Simon, I don't know how much longer we have left. We're in a reality completely different than yours or ours. We don't exist yet. Please promise us that you'll come back for us. You need to meet your wife and recreate our family tree and timeline again so that we can exist in the future here," Lộc begged.

"Listen to us Simon. I know after hearing your grandparent's stories about fleeing Việt Nam, you started to imagine a world where they never needed to do that. You even imagined a world where Việt Nam was never colonized by the French or the Chinese. And most importantly, a world where imperialist America never entered Southeast Asia and this is that reality. You have a choice to make. Do you start a fresh new life here and abandon us, or do you follow through and help us be born again into this world? We had left a liberated world to save you and it is your choice to decide your destiny," Thọ explained.

"So ultimately, it is up to me to decide. What even is the right choice? I don't want to create the wrong destiny. If I turn over a new leaf, I can carve out my own destiny. But if I recreate PLT's family tree, I can save them. It'll take several years, but if I can bring PLT back, then perhaps I can take them back to Bươm Bướm. That way I won't break both of my promises to them," Simon thought to himself. After being lost in thought, he realized that Phước, Lộc, and Thọ were already gone.

Chapter 5: Urban Legend

Simon went downstairs and found his grandparents, Lộc and Xuân, sitting at the table.

"Sài, con ăn cơm chưa?" asked Xuân.

"Chưa."

"Sài có bạn gái chưa?" inquired Lộc.

"Chưa."

"Ông bà nội có biết Bươm Bướm ở đâu không?" Simon, now referred to as Sài, asked.

"Bươm Bướm là ai?" Lộc and Xuan asked in utter confusion.

Simon was in disbelief. He wondered why Bươm Bướm wasn't in this timeline. Where could she have gone? He was sure that his grandparents would have known about the urban legend of Bươm Bướm.

～ ～

Several years had passed and Sài had decided to follow through with his promise to PLT. He eventually found his wife named Gòn. Together, Sài and Gòn had a son named Hải, who would eventually marry Thúy. Hải and Thúy had three sons named Phước, Lộc, and Thọ.

"I've been meaning to ask you three, what happened to you in the meantime while you were waiting to be born," Sài curiously asked.

"If you remember when we last used the time machine, we entered the space-time continuum and were surrounded by ocean water. Boats came towards us and turned us into cocoons and we grew butterfly wings. And yet every time we grew wings, our wings would always be cut off before we could fly to this timeline. It stung like lemon on an open wound. The only reason we were finally able to make it to this timeline was through Bươm Bướm," Phước carefully explained.

"What? How is that possible? She can't contact us unless she uses her own time machine. And plus she probably would have died from old age already right?" Sài anxiously said.

"Contrary to what you've researched and have been told, Bươm Bướm does exist in this universe. Her grave is intact and there are still four butterflies hovering over it in circles," Lộc rebuts.

"We need to go there immediately! Maybe Chanh will know something!" Sài exclaims.

Sài and PLT arrive at the grave site with four butterflies hovering over it in circles. Chanh is nowhere to be found.

"Sài, do you remember the first time you used Bươm Bướm's time machine? What happened then in the space-time continuum?" asked Thọ.

"I remember being submerged in ocean water and I heard a mysterious voice that said something in Vietnamese. I remember hearing it when you first found me and again when we tried to go to the future to reunite with Bươm Bướm. But now that I can understand Vietnamese, I know what 'chữa được bệnh, không ái chữa được mệnh' translates to now. It roughly says that 'you can cure a disease, but you cannot cure your fate.' But what does it mean though?" Sài recalls.

Sài feels a vibration in his pocket. He checks his phone to find a text from Bươm Bướm. "Look at the name of the grave."

The grave reads: "Trần Mệnh Sai." The four butterflies that were flying over the grave suddenly plummeted down to the grave, fulfilling the urban legend, and putting Simon to rest in eternal peace as he realizes he is stuck in this reality forever. Sài, Phước, Lộc, and Thọ start to fade and sink into the land once more.

Chapter 6: Wrong Destinies

"Em? Em ơi! How did you make it back to me? I thought you had died and when I heard the news, I was devastated," cried Bươm Bướm.

"It honestly felt like an eternity without you, Chị. I missed you so much," Chanh cries as she kisses Bươm Bướm. "What happened to you? You look like you've been through a war."

"Em, after Simon begged me to use my time machine to save his life from the people who were hunting him down for his activism, he died immediately from the machine. I tried to use the smell of sầu riêng to block out the smell of his corpse, but I was caught. My life was ruined. I spent several years in prison for the murder of my brother and I lost you. You were the love of my life, my Chanh, my mặt trời. After Simon's death, his comrades were inspired to continue to fight for liberation and eventually abolish the prison industrial complex, thus freeing me and giving me the proper resources I needed to recover from my years of imprisonment and the trauma of killing my brother. I spent years in therapy and I came up with this plan to change the past to be a reality where Simon never ruined my life. If my nephews successfully brought back Simon, I could put him once again in my time machine and fix everything. Simon gave me the wrong destiny and so I decided to try to change my fate," Bươm Bướm lengthily explained.

"You know, on the day that Simon died, I heard rumors that you didn't kill Simon, but rather that your time machine swapped his consciousness with the consciousness of Simon from another timeline. When I got the news that you were sent to prison, I used my spare key to your apartment to find the time machine. I used it on myself and swapped my consciousness with another consciousness of myself in the timeline that Simon went to. Your neighbors next door found my body and the news got out that I had died," Chanh laments.

"That doesn't explain how you're here though. How could you have possibly made it back to the future where I am?" Bươm Bướm wondered.

"Eventually, you sent your three nephews, Phước, Lộc, and Thọ into the past. I fabricated the "urban legend of Bươm Bướm" and lured them into my trap. Since Simon knew about our love, I knew he would try to find me like the silly goose he is. I gave him a lemon butterfly pin containing pork blood and I briefly stole their blueprints for the time machine that would've taken them to the future. I took a photo scan and then I used water to smudge their blueprint when they weren't looking. Rather than building a time machine, they built a reality machine, forcing them to go into a new reality. Then I built the time travel machine to the future and made it back here to you," Chanh sighs.

"Em, what you did was wrong. You trapped my one and only brother and my three nephews in a different reality. How could you?! Now I'll never get them back!" Bươm Bướm screams.

"I did it because I love you. I didn't want anyone or anything to tear that apart. This was the best I could do. There was no other way, my love," Chanh tightly hugs Bươm Bướm and cries.

"Chanh… I don't even know how to process this," Bươm Bướm murmurs while at a loss for words.

"Chị, listen to me. Simon ruined everything and he never approved of our love anyways. He forced you to change your destiny. Why bring him back? You have a choice to make. Live happily ever after with me in a liberated world without the toxic men in our lives or save Simon and your nephews from a reality they are stuck in? I don't even know what reality they are in. They could be in a worse reality than we are in or they could even be in something ridiculous like if imperialist America never entered Southeast Asia. You need to make a decision," Chanh demanded.

"Em. I still love you and of course I would want to pick living in a liberated world without toxic men. Yet, I don't feel that it's right for us to decide the fate of Simon and my nephews," Bươm Bướm cautiously replied.

"No one gets to decide their destiny. Don't you know the saying 'chữa được bệnh, không ái chữa được mệnh?' And who is to say that we can't decide someone else's destiny if we cannot decide ours?" Chanh laughed. "I see us as heroes carving out our own destinies, just like Hai Bà Trưng."

"Hai Bà Trưng were sisters. Em, that's weird!" Bươm Bướm exclaimed.

"I still feel like we did the right thing. Let's just live out our 'happily ever after' that we've always wanted. This society is liberated now. Everyone will accept our love and we can finally get married without fear of shame!" Chanh excitedly shouted.

"Wait Em, I need a favor from you. I need you to use the time machine one last time to go back to the past," Bươm Bướm pleaded.

"Why would I do that? We're here with each other now. Why would I throw away all of my hard work to get here?" Chanh furiously asked.

"No, I need to text Simon one last time. Each time the time machine is used, I can text Simon once," Bươm Bướm explained.

Chanh agreed and she was sent into the space-time continuum. Bươm Bướm sent a text to Simon saying "look at the name of the grave," After Chanh had fully vanished, Bươm Bướm used the machine to enter the space-time continuum.

~ ~

"Sài! What's happening?!?! Why are we sinking into the earth again?" Phước screamed.

"I have no idea!" Sài exclaimed.

"It's the urban legend!" Lộc yelled.

"No you guys. It's Bươm Bướm," calmly said Thọ.

"BƯƠM BƯỚM?!?!" they all shouted.

~ ~

"Great. Now we're ALL stuck in here. What are we suppos-" Chanh complained.

The voices of infinite ancestors and descendants within the space-time continuum all chanted, "chữa được bệnh, không ái chữa được mệnh." It felt like an eternity in an endless limbo without any means of escape.

"They're all so loud I can't even think! What do we do?" Sài yells.

"Phước. Lộc. Thọ. Do you remember what I told you many years ago about how to return home? Chant it now!" Bươm Bướm instructed.

"Uống nước, nhớ nguồn, ăn quả, nhớ kẻ trồng cây!" they all chanted vigorously with all of their hearts. Butterfly wings started to sprout from their backs and they were able to travel to the alternate reality that Chanh had trapped Sài in.

~ ~

"Bươm Bướm, thank you for saving us," Sài and PLT gratefully say.

"But aren't we now all stuck here in this reality?" Chanh complains.

"We're finally all together. This is a world where we can just live in Việt Nam in a timeline where the Vietnam War never happened. Even though Simon initially created the wrong destiny, I figured out a way to create two right destinies from it. Since I used the time machine on myself to get here, I still have a text message left to send. With one final text message, I will change Simon's destiny, " Bươm Bướm smirks

"But I'm right here?" Sài questions.

"Not you Simon, but the Simon in the original timeline," Bươm Bướm replies with a smile.

~ ~

"Britney, hurry! There isn't much time!"

"Simon, it's still a prototype! And I don't even know if it'll work!

Simon's pocket vibrates and he gets a text from an unknown sender. "Simon, this is Britney from the future. If you use this machine, you will create the wrong destiny. Liberation is possible in your lifetime. Trust me. Love, Bươm Bướm."

And Then What?

Anh-Vy Phan

"And then what?" I asked.

"What do you mean?" she looked at me curiously.

"I mean…is that it?" I pressed.

"Ngoc, everything settled after you were born. I'm not sure what you want me to say," she chuckled.

I couldn't help but hope there was more. Or, that there'd be plans for more. I stared out the window at the children laughing, holding their cups of nuoc mia. My own mouth started to salivate as I pondered how it tasted on such a hot summer day.

"But," I started, still looking out the window, "don't you wonder what's next? What lies ahead?" I asked, looking back at my mother.

Her eyes were tired. They were brown, but not the kind that are so dark that you can't differentiate between the pupil and iris. They were the kind that reminded you of a dark cup of coffee mixed with condensed milk. They were the kind that were glossy, the kind that you could get lost in. They were the kind you looked into for comfort. Nevertheless, they were tired. You'd think they wouldn't be as tired as they are, seeing as the lines surrounding them signified years of joy and happiness. When looking at my mother, you might think, "She looks fulfilled." But looks can be deceitful.

Those eyes have seen too much. They'd witness the death of their creators. Both by the hands of greedy capitalists. They'd witness the drowning of their owner's only blood relative: the owner of a similar pair of eyes, her brother. Those eyes pleaded to unsee, to not remember.

She smiled a sad smile at me as she returned to her work, organizing the dip powders on the shelf. There weren't any customers today, and she looked eager to close early. It was the Thursday before Tet, and she couldn't wait to help make loads of Banh Chung. She couldn't wait to pray to them.

"Why are you asking me about this all of the sudden? You've never asked before," she asked.

"It's just...they talked about the war today," I stared at my shoes, "and...they kept talking about us as if we were monsters, mom. It hurt, and it's confusing. I'm not sure which side I belong to."

"What do you mean?"

"I mean...I'm American, right?"

"Of course, you were born here. You're an American citizen."

"Yeah...but I'm also Vietnamese, right?"

"Of course! Why are you asking such strange questions?"

I bit my lip and continued, ignoring her question, "Right, so I'm Vietnamese but I'm also American. Which side do I choose? Am I the American soldier that went to kick Vietnam's butt in order to preserve democracy and fight communism, or am I the evil Vietnamese that threatened democracy and prosperity? Or worse, am I neither? Where do I belong then?"

My mom chuckled, "Ngoc, you're thinking about this too hard."

"Am I though, mom? When I was in class today, the teacher and my classmates turned to me when they talked about the War," I was still looking at my shoes, which were now kicking the stool to keep my emotions at bay.

"Right, probably because they know you're Vietnamese."

"Right, but when I visited Vietnam with you last summer, they called me American."

"Right, because you were born here!" she tried to explain, exasperated.

"But that's the thing mom! Don't you see? It doesn't matter where I am, there's no place where I can be whole. In America I'm the dirty Vietnamese they had to kill. In Vietnam, I'm the American who knows nothing about her culture, language, and country. No matter where I am, I'm not enough. I don't belong anywhere."

It was quiet. All that could be heard was the sound of the oscillating fan. Costco advertised it as silent. Costco, you dirty liar.

"So what are you trying to say?" mom asks, her voice shaking.

"What?" I whispered, my eyes shooting up at her. She was crying. Come to think of it, I'd never been vulnerable with my mom and expressed my thoughts and emotions like this to her before.

"Ngoc…I don't understand how you feel. Ong Ba ngoai, cau Huy and I risked our lives to escape Vietnam for a better life. And I was the only one who survived. I came here for a better chance, for a good future for you. I never imagined you'd complain about that future like this."

"Did you think that we wouldn't have problems after you settled? After you found dad and had this family?" I forced out. I wanted her to know.

"What problems? A stable education? Not living in constant fear of being shot at every 5 minutes? Being able to walk around your neighborhood without worrying about land mines? What problems, Ngoc?" she said. I could tell she was forcing too.

"Mom…" I trail off. I didn't know what to say to that.

"So you're having an identity crisis. You don't know where you belong. Geez Ngoc, at least you get to live. At least you and your brother can still hold each other. At least you still have me and Dad. At least you're safe, Ngoc. You're safe, you're stable, and you get to have a choice. I didn't, Ngoc. I didn't," she's yelling now, tears streaming down her face.

I wanted to tell her it's not just an identity crisis. I wanted to tell her the thoughts that float into my head at night. I wanted to tell her how hard it is to breathe when she and Dad tell me their random yet painful memories when they get drunk every so often. I wanted to tell her that although Hung and I can hold each other and see each other, we don't know each other. It's too painful to try.

I wanted to tell her how hard it is to get up in the morning. How when I get to school, it's hard to focus or find the drive to do anything. How my mind races when I see the water or my heart thumps a little harder and faster when I hear the sound of booming drums. I wanted to tell her that this "identity crisis" is a genuine fear. What happens when I grow up and I have my own family? And my own kids? What happens when this pain, these fears, these nightmares don't go away? What do we do? So we're settled. So we're stable. For now. What happens when we're not?

And then what?

Year of the Ox

Jennifer Hua

Tết 2021 (or Lunar New Year 2021) celebrates the Ox. The Ox is surrounded by peach trees, blooming with bright pink flowers and red lanterns (the words on the lanterns translated from Vietnamese says "happiness", "good luck" or "good fortune", and "peace"). The Ox also wears a red sash saying "Chúc mừng năm mới"—which is "Happy New Year" in Vietnamese, and a conical hat around its neck. The Ox is also holding one of my favorite desserts to eat during Tết: gelatinous rice balls filled

with mung beans, sitting in ginger syrup, topped with coconut cream, toasted sesame seeds, and minced ginger (aka "Chè Trôi Nước"). In addition, there is a Vietnamese butterfly at the top left and at the bottom, there are Chrysanthemum flowers—which are popular during Tết. Bright red and yellow or gold are believed to be the luckiest colors and bring good fortune.

Since There is No Rice

Anastasia Doanh Trinh Le

Since there is no rice, 2019, relief print, 15.5" x 15.5"

Gratitude

On behalf of 2020-2021's anthology cohort, I would like to thank you for taking your time to read our stories. These stories were born out of frustration, pain, desperation, happiness, and love. We hope that you enjoyed reading them.

Thank you so much to the Asian Pacific American Student Development office, the Southeast Asian Student Coalition Community, Southeast Asian Student Coalition alumni, members of the community for sponsoring the publication of this anthology. Without your support, this publication would not have been possible. We thank you from the bottom of our hearts for allowing our stories to be heard, shared, and loved.

To Eastwind Books of Berkeley: thank you so much for being a place where Asian Americans like ourselves can find solace and safety. Your mission of connecting the public with Asian diasporic and Asian American literature has allowed students, community members, and others to find their roots, learn more about others, and grow. Thank you for giving us the opportunity to publish with you and supporting us throughout the process.

To Professor Khatharya Um: thank you for your endless guidance and passion for leading the next generation of Southeast Asian students at the University of California, Berkeley and beyond. We appreciate you, your expertise, and your love so much.

To our families, friends, and community members: thank you for holding us, holding space for us, and loving us unconditionally. Thank you for teaching us what community and love means.

To the next generation of Southeast Asians in America: we hope you can look back at these stories one day and know that you are not alone. There are generations of us holding you. Please continue to learn about your culture, your voices, and share the gift of community and storytelling.

Again, thank you.

Alyssa Ranola

She/her/hers

Alyssa is a budding writer. She earned her bachelor's degree in English at the University of California, Davis. She served City Year for one year working in underserved schools in Sacramento and has published articles in the online paper The Tab. She currently works on her blog teaching English remotely to students living in China.

Instagram: @melodicscreams

Blog: pencilspearedhairbun.com

Anastasia Doanh Trinh Le

She/her/hers

Anastasia Le is a student at the University of California, Berkeley. When she is not studying comparative politics, she develops her poetry and printmaking practice at her other academic home, Berkeley City College. When making art, she ponders the liminal space of quiet within conflict. She is the eldest of three daughters.

Instagram: @noturstroganoff

Anh-Vy Phan

She/they/he

Anh-Vy Phan is a budding poet, artist, and polyglot at the University of California, Berkeley. They are currently double majoring in Political Science and Asian American and Asian Diaspora Studies, as well as minoring in Korean Language and Culture, in hopes of becoming a human rights and immigration attorney. When not indulging in BTS and screaming songs at the top of her lungs, Anh-Vy is snoozing or daydreaming about biting into a juicy piece of OB Town's Korean Fried Chicken.

Email: anhvyphan@berkeley.edu

Instagram: @myoongiverse.shop

Gabby Nguyen

She/her/hers

Gabby Nguyen is an undergraduate student at UC Berkeley studying psychology with interests in mental health, cognitive neuroscience, and more. She also greatly appreciates the fine arts, which can be seen in practice through her traditional portrait drawings as a freelance artist as well as her "curated" Spotify playlists that "express her feelings". In terms of academics, Gabby aspires to attend medical school to fulfill her passion for healthcare. She is currently working at a pediatric clinic and a psychiatry research lab while occasionally making time for art commissions. When Gabby isn't on the grind, she loves to snowboard, watch the sunset, and experiment in search for the perfect chocolate chip cookie recipe.

Instagram: @gabbyngu

Jennifer Hua

She/they

Jennifer Hua graduated from UC Davis with a bachelor's degree in Art Studio in 2019. Since then, she has moved back to San Diego, California and has been focusing on digital art and staying connected with the Southeast Asian community online through SEAM (Southeast Asian Mxntorship Program) as the Recruitment & Retention Coordinator. She is a fan of Day6 and Keshi music and is a part-time gamer.

Instagram: @jennqhua

Phibi Tran

They/them

phibi tran is a queer, non-binary diasporic Vietnamese person in America, author of the short story Simon - Wrong Destiny. Originally from Little Saigon San Diego, phibi came to the Bay Area a few years ago for education and organizing. They are a graduating senior from UC Berkeley with a double major in Cognitive Science & Asian American and Asian Diaspora Studies. Outside of academics, phibi does community organizing with Queer and Transgender Asian American collectives and organizations. phibi's experiences in academia and organizing shaped their political frameworks and inspired some of the themes within their short story. Learning Vietnamese was also a critical shift in how they processed the world and gave them more words to create art with. In their spare time, they do ribbon dancing, graphic design, cooking, and traveling. Simon - Wrong Destiny is their first major work and was inspired by philosophical theories, video games, conversations about Vietnamese leftist politics, and their own personal life experiences. phibi's future projects involve more ribbon dancing, exploration of their Southeast Asian and queer identity, as well healing work. Over the next few years, they will be applying to graduate school to become a Licensed Professional Clinical Counselor and practice in their local community.

Instagram: @phibeanie

Prinston Pan

He/him

Prinston Pan is a Laotian American born in Kansas and is currently a high school junior in Southern California. He uses his poetry to raise awareness about the history of Laos. He enjoys swimming, travelling, and spending time with friends and family.

Riss Myung

She/her/hers

If Riss lived in Avatar the Last Airbender, she would be a word bender. Influenced by multigenerational sisterhood, she shapes syllables and words to tell stories -- chapters that collect the truths in her individual to societal systemic experiences. A transnational anti-imperialist feminist, she finds her writing and poetry rooted in not just her past, but the history of the women who resisted and rose before her. She hopes that her words will continue to pave the way for the future generation to walk across a clearer, more paved path. Riss herself is on a journey to become the best possible version of herself.

Instagram: @myung.sisters

Twitter: @risspeaks